PICTURES
FROM A RESERVATION

PICTURES
FROM A RESERVATION

Gerard Reidy

DEDALUS PRESS
DUBLIN, IRELAND

First published in 1998
This edition published in 2008
The Dedalus Press
13 Moyclare Road
Baldoyle
Dublin 13
Ireland

www.dedaluspress.com

ISBN 978 1 904556 24 7

Dedalus Press titles are represented in North America
by Syracuse University Press, Inc., 621 Skytop Road,
Suite 110, Syracuse, New York 13244, and in the UK by
Central Books, 99 Wallis Road, London E9 5LN

Cover painting by Dermot Seymour

The Dedalus Press receives financial assistance from
An Chomhairle Ealaíon / The Arts Council, Ireland

Contents

September

Autumn, and the drowsy gods
have woken late.
They met Bacchus at a house party —
now they pull the curtains and curse.
The Atlantic is uneasy, knows what to do
but waits for the command.
Our stream is still dry, however,
reports are reaching me that
sometime last night a flowerpot was overturned
and in suburbia a garden gate swung open.
The artist, wild-eyed, is cycling
down towards the harbour where out at sea
the clouds have lined up like great
destroyers, battling with the feeble sun.

On the river bank golden willows
like pompom girls are ready
to introduce the first flood to the town.
At the vegetable market confusion is perfect:
An upturned stall and the crush
of grapes and cabbage.
In the stillness after rain
breathe in, breathe in.

Deirdre

We meet on the landing
with our nightmares intact;
your favourite doll became a tiger
in the bed beside you

while I found you face down
in the flooded stream.
You piggy-back downstairs
silently fastened to me.

Then you chase a surprised beetle
on all fours down the hall.,
It escapes between floorboards.
A single tear runs down your cheek.

In the kitchen, having cereal,
I read yesterday's paper
and you direct a drama
between the knife and the spoon.

We cross the road to the pier
barefooted in the sun,
the springtide slowly filling,
wavelets slurping under our feet.

With our backs to the world
we dream and gaze out to sea
at Achill's windows reflecting
under a Paul Henry sky.

The milkman garrulous as usual
breaks the silence :
"She's going to be a scorcher."
We trot back into the house.

I know this will never happen again.
You cry when your hair is combed.
I straighten my tie, suppress a tear
and the world closes slowly in.

Dreaming of Paddy Flaherty

Today was another day flavoured with
rusty quays in the east of England.
Where tall weeds intimidate black children
playing beside derelict cranes,

on which the company's name
mocks the employees' brick houses.
Where retired sailors watch kids
and seagulls in the polluted stream.

The ice-cream man reads the *Mirror*
as the North Sea fog moves inland.
Teenagers make furtive love in the sand dunes
beside a Coke tin and dried cow dung.

Paddy is senile in the clinical home,
longs to immerse himself in anarchy
outside the empty halls and perfect grounds
and dreams of a fair day in Connemara.

He first put his hand on her thigh
while watching Bing Crosby in the temperance hall.
Later a monkey puzzle grew in their garden
and the kids ate cereal with real wheat germ.

On the annual holiday in Brighton
with pain in his civil-war eyes he applied
lotion on her freckled back. She could be
the lady on the cereal pack with a free beachball.

Beside the ice-cream shed he imagines a radio –
the inevitable Galway-Mayo football match
on a Sunday evening in 1935 as you ask me
for the third time to pass the salt in 1985.

Just Another Gale

"Breezy up along these western coasts,"
the English forecast said,
conceding that we too have
weather in the Republic.
Outside a gale blows through the graveyard.
Overlooking Killary Harbour
the headstones whistle a tune
that nobody listens to.
Even the humble hawthorn
is forced to kiss the ground.
Fleeting moonlight reflects
off distant mountain lakes.
A stone wall crumbles beside a tree
and guilty sheep break into a meadow.
The clouds are phantoms that caress
and gallop over drumlins.
There's a worried candle queue
in McGuire's shop where parents
relive a wartime courtship. They claim
sweeter pints by oil lamp,
even the fiddle and banjo sound better
and in the game of cards the night's
kitty has gone missing.

When the power is restored
there comes a cold sense of purpose.
The morning challenge to school and work
leaves us weaving through Blue Bangor slates.

In the bustle of Portobello Road
a Cockney ice cream lady smiles
as a whirlwind of litter
gathers beside a sleeping Labrador.
Street traders stack up flower pots.
Blues records nod forward without fuss.
In the Home Counties
excited gardeners are praying
that this breeze might bring some rain.

Light Years

On Christmas Eve who was I
to explain a shooting star?
They were determined to believe
that magic was on its way.
For this was a privileged moment
in the formation of a half-remembered childhood.
Next day snow fell heavily and we
tobogganed as the carols demanded.

You remember how, after opening
silage pits, he would stop the car,
hop stones off the ice on Holland's Lake –
our tinselled moment
in the ballast of childhood memories.

Now after decades wandering
in a self-imposed desert I,
for a brief moment, almost felt included.
One must travel through the night
to see shooting stars.

November Day

On mornings like these
we disturbed the red white-heads
content as the hares played
and crows perched on their backs.

We marched them to the gate
through a pocket of dawn fog.
The neighbour's cattle curious
followed them to a field corner.

They leaped and raced down the road,
sentries posted at all the gaps.
A pigeon fluttered in the hedge,
and they were scared into the bog

Bikes abandoned in the briars
we leaped over the ditch
and galloped up the hill
as the train from Westport trundled by.

At the crossroads we'd meet McHale
leading a dry cow with a halter,
his black suit shiny with time,
laden with his mother's instructions.

Our space is outside Mrs Murphy's house.
Her window sill collected dung pyramids.
Under the town clock we saw geese peer
sideways through holes in canvas bags.

One day we met coming from the fair
Gillespie, riding the mare with the cart
empty behind, McHale sleeping in the Volkswagen
with the calf sucking his ear.

Suspended on a bar stool in McGing's
I saw a pale winter sunshine discover
cornflakes and bags of oats,
as an old woman chewed tobacco under the stairs.

Among the dark angular figures
my father is paid a few notes
peeled from a wad of twenties
with Davitt's ghost smiling everywhere.

Inside Out

We stopped near Crewe
on the boat train to London
and gazed through the night sky
at the countless hospital patients.
When our eyes made contact, mother,
I said nothing but you knew --

Later that year
you shuffled up beside me
saying "I'll soon be as tall as you"
and laughed a laugh that meant
nothing and everything.
I saw your eyes in the mirror
vacant and finally unshackled,
eyes dancing like a teenager
asking me was I married.
You reassured me with silence
and approving nods until one morning
you sat in the kitchen protesting
while spreading coffee on the bread.
Halloween fell on Ash Wednesday
and Bonfire Night on New Year's Day.
Your dress sense became fashionable.

My father never said a word.
Just worked forty years
to have his petty pension taxed
and tore milk sachets
into machine coffee every day
in the hospital canteen
and battle with a plastic knife
against a microwaved bun,
gazing unfocused over the Coca-Cola
dispenser at the waves of seagulls
on the Corporation tiphead.

For several months I was armed
until one day when the train had passed
you said nothing but I knew.
When our eyes made contact
you mumbled from the vortex
of your memory "Don't forget to
say a prayer, it's Good Friday"
and it was.

Twilight Zone

On this cold February day
the pipe is being laid in the earth's wound.
Snow concedes to the black clay
like bubbles falling to the ground at dawn.

The whistle goes, the men fade,
retreating from the jaws of earth.
What right have we to do this was heard.
They joked instead of Reilly's speeding fine.

In the hut, sausages burn on coals
which thaw the frozen hearts of steel.
Outside the surgeon's knives heal,
each stitch a screaming manhole.

Their wives wheel prams on potholed roads
and brave the heathen wind in winter sunshine.
Sleet showers move down from Dublin hills;
thighs shown to boys in the broken telephone box.

He comes home to be smothered by children,
parish newsletter still stuck in the letterbox.
Outside the day is strangled from the east
as the neon lights flicker in distant Tallaght.

Brush Strokes (after Seurat)

There's a stray donkey on the bog road.
Sheep's wool blows from barbed wire.
Cows, drunk with grass, doze in midsummer heat.
Briars snail through windows of a Morris Minor,
while nettles investigate the engine.

The Ferguson's perished tyres
leave dust clouds on the lane
as cocks of hay are swept in.
The hired driver is an accepted hero
rewarded by the largest steak at lunchtime.

The tractor engine is the focal point
where bottles of Christmas stout are drunk.
"Ah it's not the same as the counter", says Ward.
The sheepdog tilts his head to a muffled sound –
the first threshing machine of the season.

In the village, they are dipping sheep
with ritual, oriental gaiety.
They uncovered a gladiator at Pompeii;
in Woodquay they found the Vikings.
In Mayo they'll discover a bachelor
saving hay.

Morning At St. Jude's

And finally the rain came
an hour before dawn.
Its music in the gutter
washed away the tension.
The moon chased out the bay,
hid behind an island.
All night I was restless
as the blue voltage of sudden death
leaked into every room.

In the car park at the central bank
pregnant trees lost branches.
The executive, too, was delayed
opening his office four minutes late.
Old men grinned and complained
it wasn't forecast.

That night the gods took photographs
and the handicapped girl at the
bay window in her dormitory
was smiling every time.
When the rain finally came.

About Rhyme And Other Things

The mayor is proud of the new town park,
his chain shines in the parade.
When his daughter plays in the band
her smile is a valley in May.

Radiant girls play tennis
while boys fit on uniforms.
Mothers plant out geraniums while dads
cut grass outside the perimeter fence.

Inside, life is different, with its neat piles
of shoes, glasses and crutches.
Summer forms a sweet smell in the chimney,
fog gathers in the orchard.

The television insists that we're all
cutting grass at the perimeter fence.
Some still ask why this poem can't rhyme
like Bosnia, Cambodia and Rwanda.

Rhythms

My car is abandoned
at the disused quarry,
I sit by the lake
as slivers of moonlight are washed up
at the ruined boathouse.

I want to dissolve forever
into this limestone wall.
I envy the cooling rock
under relaxing sycamores.
The cuckoo calls perfectly.

Mountains drown in haze.
Cattle grazing on the hill are
a camel caravan on the horizon.
I imagine tribesmen etched
into the railway bridge.

A wind-bitten whitethorn
becomes a drought stricken acacia.
Overtaken by tribal rhythms
I dance around the bonfire
until the solstice dawn.

Being servant of Stonehenge
and Newgrange I rotate.
As victim of weather
I dance to the tyranny
of its current affairs.

For days now in this heat
I've been paddling a dugout
on your ritual Congo.
The clergy are performing
what could be called a raindance.

Before Demolition

They never locked the front door,
left suits in the wardrobes,
wedding photos on the walls,
a calendar from '57.
The front porch tiles were strewn
with *Readers' Digest*, final notices.
The half-empty marmalade jar
waits beside a postcard from Chicago
on the cluttered oilcloth table
in October evening lambency,
preserved like Scott's last meal
before heading out for the Pole,
and the sink — blocked with potato skins
as it was the day my mother
left home.

Endurance

Why aren't the Christmas crowds applauding
as a harvest moon comes up Talbot Street?
Why aren't the fish in Clew Bay pirouetting
as a shower is entangled in sun over Achill?
Why aren't the sheep in the amphitheatre of Doolough
giving a Mexican wave to the vortices of water?
Why aren't the stars spelling our names
and the planets competing to be full stop?
Why must I wrestle every day with that image
of the dawn etching our naked embrace?
Why must I carry this image to the shore
like a drunk who met an angel and forgot her address?

Lecanvey

I sit, numb on the pier.
A depression over the continent
brings easterlies from Russia.
The sea retreats, waves protest.

Distant Nephin appears as if caught
in a permanent snowdrift
and radiates its indifference
to Croagh Patrick.

As the Ice Age retreated
I imagine its pagan core never thawed.
Its chain of peaks to the West
forms a snow curtain against the Atlantic.

I dream of Dr. Zhivago far to the East
snowbound in his winter palace
looking out across the moonlit steppe
at the wolves howling on the hillside.

Tchaikovsky's overture
like a trans-Siberian express
racing along in a great tide
of upheaval and euphoria.

But here in Lecanvey
I can't ignore a black Anglia
as it engulfs a ribbon of road
on its way to first mass.

The Dispossessed

What's an old man for,
but to wave feebly at a toddler,
screaming through the mesh wire
of a corporation garden fence?

To swing his hand
on the way to a pound shop
to buy a useless toy
in the early Saturday markets?

To realise his dreams
with an old car bonnet in the snow
or to show him where to find mushrooms
and how to gather them on a wisp?

What's a toddler for,
but to wave back
at the old man blinded
by an eddy of leaves in autumn?

To look under the bed
in the blinding sunshine for his shoes
as he straightens his back
and the funeral bell rings?

To scream during Sunday mass
allowing them both to escape
to his local and to walk
home along the riverbank?

What are we for but to pay homage
to the dispossessed and celebrate
their simplicity? Loose slates will never
bother me again on stormy nights.

January Evening

The dark curtain coming down
and he's standing on the pedals.
Cycling towards a gap where
the bony cow stood all day.

She follows him down the road,
delighted in the rain, past the lame bull,
and waits in her own place
to be tied in the old house.

The ritual begins, rope for the tail,
a saucepan for the cat,
and the back door blows in
with a gust of hail from the north.

The boots parked beside
the blackened Stanley range.
His mother's eyes rolling in prayer
as he reads "Old Moore's Almanac".

On the mantelpiece a cracked cup
half full of rusty staples
and the butcher's warped calendar
behind her pink broken glasses.

During the rosary he reads
about the county final
and hears the echo of wild geese
flying to the mountain corrie.

She empties the chamber pot.
He turns his boots.
She fills the hot water bottle.
They retire without a word.

Outside there is the symphony
of a rainbarrel overflowing.

The Soul Agents

Every day I watch you withdraw
into the security of a shadow.
The young years deflated with guilt
which you must carry 'till the end.
Despite protests, life, you say,
must focus on the approaching
wail of a cemetery gate
in the March east wind.
For you, glass falling
from a rotting window after frost
is an event, winter's
flowering cherry a bad omen.
In November you're at home
pointing to the future,
anxious to press the ashes
onto the skin in Lent.

I button my coat
in the teeth of your nuclear winter.
Through the spears of your
local radio and parochial pawns
I can barely discern the sap
rising in the woods, in spring..

The salmon moving upstream
are heavy-eyed with thoughts of spawning.
I hear a handbrake turn
between the hills after a disco.
We're numb when the exams are over
when we charge batteries with lead solos.
Houses reckless in summer,
their shadows surprising students
sleeping in tents after the rock festival.

Hendrix play for us
Morrison play for us
Pink Floyd play for us
Dylan play for us.

Rhubarb bursts open
in the back yard of a small town
through ashes and broken glass
beside the disused railway track.
A butterfly invades a dead
solicitor's house on main street.
A German hiker accepts a lift
in the transport box of a tractor.

The grey figures of ageing men
turn off the main road
cycling to the bog,
jubilant, lunches on the carrier.
Children twist their toes
on the softened tar.
The master plays in goal
even in my old school yard.

Bent with the old baggage,
have you not seen your deranged congregation,
with holes where their eyes used to be,
sawing up the pews for use as truncheons,
queuing up to ring your funeral
with an electronic bell,
cutting barbed wire from around your neck
and trying to murder you
with the clear blue light of freedom.

Paddy From Ballycroy

I passed you at the ball alley
smoking Woodbines, in turned down boots, wet.
A whisky bottle hid under your coat —
the kind we brought our milk to school in.

"How did the headage go?" I asked.
"They were all passed.
Ward is bringing them home
in the trailer," you said.

You went home to read the tabloids
to the sound of local radio
and the call of hens.
Your fiddle silent on the wall.

There too, sellotaped pictures
of Pope John, JFK, Marilyn Monroe,
first holy communion, and the sacred heart
burning like you in the fading light.

Your parents' room never opened
since her frail figure was carried away.
Her half-full Vick's cough bottle
is still standing.

I remember the night you died
beside a young solicitor's car.
Your bicycle lamp shining
faithfully into the wet mud.

His girl friend shivered when she saw
the rib steak fallen from the saddle,
mixing its blood with yours
on the fresh wet gravel.

Bedroom at Dawn

Those years I see you, Tom,
strapped to your car child seat,
facing the wrong way,
waving recklessly as my train pulled out
and your mother's car weaving
past the smoking dump
and the Readymix concrete plant
in a watery October sunshine.
Damming the stream in August
waiting to challenge the autumn rains
you coaxed the high tide
all the way to our doorstep.

I savour this perfect moment at daybreak.
A cloud cradled under Croagh Patrick,
the dawn chorus outside your window,
as sunlight spills into your room.
The tadpoles you rescued from the turlough
wriggle in slimy jam jars, your chestnut seeds
just emerging as swallows compete to build
under your window.

In winter storms — when all seems lost,
the full moon of your face like a ripening
field of oats reflects
almost forgotten perfect summers.

Echoes

I visit tourist resorts off season
to listen to summer echoes.
At Bertra sheep graze around toilets.
Ice tissues marooned pools.
A dying ass is covered by blown sand.

In Spain apartments are being built
along the sea front.
Dampness invades ice-cream shacks.
Sewer pipes lie on a rain-soaked beach.
Flies mate in souvenir shops.

Snow stays late on shaded balconies.
Madrid is consumed in a soft drizzle.
Atlantic weather roars in over Europe
and oh the beauty of Leningrad
just after the river freezes.

We drive home with no real purpose
through cities to our town,
its streets in pale autumn sunshine
and a sheep fair on the mall
leaves me wandering in aimless delight.

The Gap Is Closing

He cuts gorse bushes with a bow saw.
He brings his lunch,
the milk bottle corked with paper.
He plods home across the fields at dark
along the silent river
and latches the timber gate.

He's bursting with boyish happiness; I surprise him.
"It's going to freeze hard tonight,
I know by the sound of the train", he says.
After milking the frisian he scolds her manners.
As he drinks his cup of tea and eats his bread
I know his work is his religion.

We couldn't agree on the colour of a blue sky.
But in recent years I find myself
changing into his gear before the railway bridge,
driving long straight roads in third
and at the junction wiping fog
off my side window
in exactly his ominous shape.

Connemara Colours

October cloudswirl in a wild red sky.
Birds are tangled in gusts of golden leaves.
A curlew screams in joyous frenzy.
Drains are filled with brown floods.

On a lonely road near Leenane
a gipsy girl with auburn hair
wrapped in disorder around her face
turns her head, catches my eye

and licks the pouring rain from her lips.
I must recoil to where the first snow lies
left like a child at mass, gazing
at a spray of sunlight through stained glass.

Slievemore Deserted Village

Curlew calls over the lake
as the rain clears.
Brittle wisps hiss, like
phone wires to an island.
Low cloud communicates
with famine ridges.

And in the ruins, I imagine
thin limbs of victims
outstretched to bridge the time.
In shame I retreat alone.
Their grandchildren ageing gracefully now
in Pennsylvania and Chicago.

Diminished grass is slowly consumed.
Rushes enjoy a sinister revenge.
Their creeping paralysis ruthless
even in the most sacred places.
In the distance a figure approaches,
stumbles across the bog onto a track.

He disappears now and then in the hollows.
Smoked like a Moroccan street trader
he offers me a load of breast turf,
as if boatloads of grain wouldn't leave the quay,
as if magpies wouldn't pick our eyes out,
as if grass wouldn't melt in our mouths.

Wish You Were Here

As a child, I adored the sun.
Then one day I watched
as thunderclouds
like giant oil tankers
developed in the east,
queued outside our gable.
As we were counting the sheep
the last sun rays
escaped over the Atlantic.
The shadow crept over,
the sun strangled,
darkness came, then silence.
Dad went skeleton pale.
Mother was armed with Holy Water.
After the first crack
I felt a shiver.
It was that day
the child fled,
words were measured.
I was gladly taken
from under the apple tree,
across the Rhine and the Volga
and finally over the Urals
to where I now rest,
in the serenity of Siberian plains.

Fellow Mammal

A solitary bulb swings,
liquid shadows rotate.
A saw rips through your bones.
Chops and Sunday roasts
bagged and labelled.

Last week in the turf shed
you smelled blood flowing.
Betrayal your last bleat.
The severed body shuddered.
The nervous voltage earthed.

"There's no length in the day now," says McHale.
"Did you let out the ram yet?" says Ward.

Eight months ago you slid into the world,
survived hailstones, magpies, greybacks
to see endless summer days,
playing between whitethorns,
diminished earth banks,

or scared of your shadow
in the flood after the storm.
You lived our lifetime
without calendar or diary
or the fear of death.

Bright Spells And Scattered Showers

I'm sifting through old schoolbooks
in my father's disused cowshed.
Physics, Virgil and algebra,
notated in old Irish.

He throws *De Bello Gallico* on the fire,
the handwriting over the Latin
peels in the flame and I'm sucked away
to years of twilight evenings in the back room,

to see the still life of familiar
cheese, folders and beer bottles
on a cluttered formica table
in a basement Salthill flat.

I came home on a sleepy bus
letting off pensioners at every crossroads.
That summer after the last exam
the locals wondered why I was happy footing turf.

Marooned again in that back room
found gaping through a window
onto a cracked yard, another day
of bright spells, scattered showers.

Another Sense

Night, the hall, a presence,
like a rabbit aware of its shadow
caught in the car headlights,
I was consumed by forces.

I could hear a range creaking next door.
A downpipe dripping after rain.
McGuire's rusty bow-saw
falling from a hook in the barn.

Morning, between the curtains of an old nightclub,
dust is surprised in a cylinder of sunlight.
A showband poster dissolves in rising damp.
A nettle grows through a window.

Outside, a Monet haze envelops the lake,
cows idle in the water,
frogspawn vibrate with life,
weeds embrace each other for support.

I would like to know on what day the winter's ended,
which wave marks the tide's change,
the exact angle of the rain
when the donkey turns his rump to the wind.

Greeting a Spring Storm

Beyond the car park wall
masts nod in a high tide.
They beckon to me like circus dinosaurs
as a gale fills up the bay.
Impatient they seem to parade
in the docks enclosure
and nudge against the pier
pointing to the horses out at sea.
Like trains in a station
I can't be sure who's moving.
A boy marches through cobbled streets
gazing into the middle distance,
the fishing rod firmly clenched;
his mother calls after him in vain.

The spring sky illuminates
like some great celestial torch —
the derelict coastguard station,
the itinerants washing their children,
the hawkers outside the cattle mart,
the County Council workers lighting oil lamps,
the cross-eyed dump caretaker

McHale cleaning the cow shed,
the Down's Syndrome girl
sitting in her wheelchair,
a string of sausages
inside the butchers' window,
the barber's shop with its
pictures of football teams,
a traffic warden adjusting his tie,
the Chinese cook cheering his son
in the sack race.

I put on the bicycle clips,
call the dog and head for home
pedalling through the seagulls
into the wind, past the crowd
at the cinema, for a while
happier than any man I know.

Polish Master

The last frost before summer
enchanted the sheep fencing.
I can still see *Paradise Lost*
peeping from my school bag on the bus.

It happened at this place
where starved donkeys followed a farmer
plodding through churned mud
across fields to a ditch.

I was sitting beside the girl
with the shortest skirt.
Her powers were for once earthed.
Your piano haunted me all day.

Since then, topping rushes
or factory work doesn't bother me.
That day I was released
with your Ballade No.1 in G.

Frozen Memories

In silence the ponds were locked.
Swans whirred low towards the sea.
A dusting of snow fell sadly
as night clutched the last sunrays
from the abandoned plains.

During school breaks we climbed the walls
and piled stones on frozen lakes
to make a dull rock music.
Old Hughes laughed as we collapsed
or ran aground at an island of rushes.

On Carra they hunted the pike
by breaking holes in ice.
Some men waited decades for this frost.
It could have been the Great Bear Lake
fished by Eskimos.

Memories flood back on a summer evening
in pathetic drizzle I gaze into the distance
beside closed public toilets
while on a caravan holiday in Lahinch
while Segovia plays Albeniz on the radio.

Last House Before The Bog

He hears the flood approaching
and parks his car the far side of the bridge.
Born beside the great river and the unnamed lake
he can never live in the housing estate.

He knows his own ewe in a hundred,
outwits the dealer every year in buying sheep.
Germans looking for sites are hooked
by a special twinkle in his eye.

He shows me which turf bank to cut,
where water trickles over a broken kesh
and distant nomadic goats wander in the heat,
their favourite sun-traps turned green with use.

He looks at the sky urgently
and limps over the hill with the dog
to leave me with echoes of Civil War ambush
and clatter of Norman bone on a stony hillside.

I love his incorrect, dismantled cars
suspended on blocks, plastic bags of coal,
yellow gas bottles used as goal posts,
and silage bales, all in the front garden.

This annual pilgrimage is a cleansing,
a distant memory on November nights,
like gazing into the void between ship and quay
or sampling the names of Siberian towns.

But on other nights I'm out there with you
your distant homes huddled in the storm
and wind stripping peat from the mountains.
It's then I turn on my side and pray for pale morning.

Waiting Rooms

I saw them going to the college cider party,
the judge's daughter on the handlebars,
with fashionable pint glass stains
on her applied maths notes.

They wore shoe leather for Allende,
waved Mao's red book at me,
played Neil Young songs by the fire,
even wore carnations in their hair.

I wished I had a sheep's head to hang
in the living room as protest
when the old caretaker remarked that in time
even they would exploit Dylan for consumption

in their chain stores, banks and waiting rooms.
The clergy would bless their extensions
and safe landscapes would be hung
inside corporate double glazing.

Now, in the queue I'm ambushed
by laundered versions of Lennon, Hendrix
and imagine hanging on their walls —
airbrushed impressions of Guernica,

a gay schoolgirl in a graveyard
giving birth under a statue,
cattle dismembered at a factory,
a carefree driver collecting heads and hearts,

merry itinerants playing in the town dump
approved by the knowing smiles of clean wise rats,
Jews in a mid-war sing-song
travelling east in cattle trucks.

Reflections

I sit in the empty car park watching
the street festival across the river.
I can hear an autumn flood
gathering around the salmon weir,
the lunchtime concert in "Smokey Joe's",
the tired maths lecturer juggling
Greek symbols on a screen,
and the tinkle of Spanish boats
sheltering in the docks.
Again I'm in the centre of it all,
a Tuam woman looking for Dunnes Stores,
students sampling each other's accents,
the market smell on Saturday mornings.
Like an astronaut returning to New York after fallout
I wander into lecture theatres,
crowded bars with traditional music,
and hear echoes of characters
from a Breughel painting.
I take the boat out on the lake
and gaze back at the busy college
as swans pass by under the castle.
On a narrow street I meet a boy with a T-square
determined to draw straight lines in only one colour.
On this pleasant afternoon during college week
I sit in the empty car park watching
the street festival across the river.

Skyscape

After our first encounter
I was lost.
Your swirling colours leave me
walking into lamp-posts.

I greet your summer storms
lying down on grassy hillsides
and the frost on the East wind
while chopping turnips with a spade.

For years now I've been drunk
admiring your changing canvas.
The wicked games you play with our seasons
can be forgiven.

Often you have punished
with your tyranny of westerlies.
Then you send me showers
to challenge the setting sun

and I'm frozen on the spot by your panorama;
I must gather the fencing tools.
A Fiat farts over the hill to the town festival.
Again I promise to worship you.

The Past Approaching

As I drove home that Friday evening
the sun broke through in the west
as it did in our national school.
It was like Swiss music on an old wireless,

like finding your favourite racing car
when digging the garden,
like grandfather's picture on the piano --
the light from a burnt out star.

I was trying to cross the road
of south-bound civil servants
anxious to get into their denims
and drive an ancient tractor.

At home my brother has discovered
live rounds in an old barn.
My father's remorse concerning
a buried mass rock grows daily.

On frosty nights I hear echoes
from our local ruined ballroom.
I can almost touch the tip
of Hitler's outstretched hand.

Night Sketches

I

On this calm August night
fog surrounds an empty house
and ghosts are free to roam
through nettles and broken crockery,
cookers and cracked Bovril jars.
The cloud confuses the mountain
and the river is confined to its banks.
Potato stalks lurk behind the hedge.
Scattered whitethorns on the horizon
are the masts of sleeping ships.

II

But then the Gods become uneasy
and the moon must reveal itself
when a breeze flows down the valley.

III

And in our house by the graveyard
where the school bus is parked on the hill,
the name from a neighbour's headstone
is slowly being reflected
on the ceiling of my bedroom.
Pigeons cry uneasily in the
tall branches of the plantation
and tree shadows score the garden.
Behind an upturned Volkswagen
dew drops glow on barbed wire.

IV

In the distance I see a back kitchen light,
empty Budweiser cans on a formica table
and Ward asleep on the clinker of a dead fire.

Another Life

I've queued here in March east wind
when snow flurries filled dry potholes
and on summer bank holidays
when tourists drove the other way.
Our trucks leave trails of piss
outside souvenir shops which
causes a resolution to be
passed at the Urban Council meeting.
Outside the hawkers who
could be from Kabul
offer me four Jim Reeves tapes
and a complete set of spanners for a tenner.
At the sale ring a dealer
puts his arm around me and bids
with the reassurance of a friendly cow
shitting politely in my wellington.
He tells me, "Ryan's bull
dismantled the trailer
at the traffic lights in Ballina.
He sent him to the factory
only got the price of a cow."
Tired calves are weaned
beside their mothers with pea tins
strapped to their mouths. Auctioneers

scared of silence compose
their own language. The car radio
emits races from Naas
as a cow is casually dehorned in the pen.
In the canteen flies copulate
in diluted sauce bottles
Oxtail soup condenses, and drips
from the ceiling. Prices are marked
up to the nearest pound.
Cigarette boxes float, confidently
in canals of rasher scented urine.
A tow bar has introduced itself
to a buyer's car from Limavaddy,
I have examined marts from all sides
like a farmer wrestling with a round rock;
they leave me bruised, upended,
but one winter's night, coming from Dublin
I parked up as chilly dawn approached.
The man in the mobile canteen —
just like in the old fair days —
was still cutting half-crown ham sandwiches.

Spring

Your freight train has
ambushed our valleys
on its way north.
The spectre dissolves.
The last hailstones
make a futile protest
outside a Salthill shop.
Pressure battles are over.
Cows blinded by sunlight,
driven from dung-caked barns.
Muddy fields behind the shed
hardened, tall weeds colonise.
A farmer carries a French girl
and bags of meal from the store.
Frost hides behind the hills and
skulls are crushed by tractor wheels.
Sheep carcasses on the mountain
are discovered after snow melts.
The last rope of hay is sadly
abandoned in the garden.
Croagh Patrick's blue teepee
sends cumulus signals
in carefree celebration
to the men footing turf.

I switch off the tractor
and admire the parade.
Locked in dark lakes, I know
grey backs attack young lambs.
Around now the city is unsafe.
Out here, in the heave of fresh vegetation,
the shelter of asylum beckons
souls with fissured childhoods.

Dancing Alone

The day my mother died
fish jumped into nets
and boats docked at the airport.
The river flowed up Main Street
and disappeared through a needle's eye.
After three days of darkness
the sun came up in the North,
stopped over our house for an hour
and set like a comet in the East.
A Goddess knocked on the back door
and led me away, away, away.
Years later while walking home
in the pouring rain at midnight,
I shed one measured tear
for all the world to see
how difficult it was to dance alone.

The Reservation

Small farmers panic over crops,
while my country bleeds alone,
like a hit-and-run victim at night
forgotten in the midsummer heat.

When I turn in for winter,
your parish festival leaves me cold.
Our kids have bought one-way tickets,
determined to find bright colours.

Your streets await innocent tourists
who, we desperately hope, will stay
to pollute us when we are purified
by the Chinese drop of church and state.

In their sad puppet show
we must hold onto strings
like tin soldiers at the funfair
mechanically playing our own music.

We know our fate is sealed --
not to wait for the contractor's pick-up
at seven a.m. on Kilburn High Road,
but to cash the headage cheque

and sell the donkey's harness
to the Irish pub in Shanghai,
or wait to be chosen as extras
like the Sioux in a cowboy film.

The Call

I

You're silhouetted
against the kitchen window
seated beside yesterday's supper dishes.
In your hospital dressing gown
you shiver with the January cold.
A palm tree waves in the gale.
The Africa magazine is folded
under the leg of the table.
False teeth are partially submerged
in the dirty margarine tub.
Your mouth out of control now,
as you count tablets on a china plate
and wait for the death notices
to be read on local radio.
Whispering the rosary,
anticipating a passing car.
From the cracked glass
a purse of water grows on the window sill.

II

A pale sun reveals branches
waving on faded wallpaper.
You gaze at a hole in the floor
where marbles used to gather
or at a photo of a dead grandchild
between the covers of a prayerbook.
You're still cooking for two,
feeding the hens with scraps
of Kentucky fried chicken..
A donkey brays on the hill,
light reflects off the school bus
as it turns the crossroads.
You check the winter time :
it's exactly an hour fast.
Your pines brace themselves
as a curtain of hail
sweeps in from the coast.

III

A candle is ready for the power failure,
The wind sucks at your bedroom window
and a distant rumble of thunder
causes you to check
with the Sacred Heart.

Pictures look down on you,
sisters, parents and husband
beckoning from summer photographs,
anniversaries, parties and weddings.
You wake to the sound of teenagers
throwing stones at your empty hayshed.
A flash of blue lightning captures
the barn's fallen roof,
the harness perched on rafters,
the outline of your skull.
The light goes out, then nothing.
The telephone rings.

Girls from 1984

I thought time had something to do with
appointments, clocks, calendars,
mature reflections on the passage of a life
until, one day, beautiful women in white coats
came to collect me when I was photocopying
plans for the sewage treatment plant in Achill.
When they tucked me in and folded
a second pair of pyjamas in my locker
hung up their coats I could see
reflected in the bathroom mirror
printed on their skin-tight tee-shirts
as the morning shift arrived
If you are not living on the edge
you are just a waste of space.
But I am, I protested, living on the edge —
and continued with my work as usual.

Lankill Blues

We parked the bicycles beside the turfstack,
robbed Ned Murphy's apples and ran
with Carson through the meadow,
but it wasn't like that.
His parents didn't go to mass
so he had to stay ourside alone
eating his lunch in the school shelter.
The January rain
wriggled down window panes
disguising tears inside when
you beat ten shades of crap
out of us -- which one day
gathered in Patricia's boots.
After hours in the sobbing gloom
you paid her to be sick
the day of the catechism test.
When Mrs. Quinn heard the silence
you knew it was too late.
We had no cotton to pick
or slide guitars to strum
outside a timber shack,
only Muddy Waters playing
on a scratched record at bedtime.

There were events in later years —
when Ellen smacked your face
at the guards' dinner dance,
the builder in London
feebly looking for a vein
swore he would take revenge
mumbling to himself outside
the fluorescent washed take away.
Well Pat, you'll be glad to know
we're nearly as balanced as you were
and when you shook my hand
smiling confidently at the reunion,
I was left wailing in the darkness
still impaled on your bayonets
of love and trust.

Daytrip - for Eleanor

Late winter sunshine
soothed the yellow hills.
A whisper of wind
rippled the bog lake.

The sheltered inlet reeked
with a silence
of lichens and upturned boats,
car wrecks and craft shops.

The whitewashed *Times Square*
video shop was suspended
over the shore, flanked
by withered nettles in the cracked pavement.

Vacant suburbia was occupied only
by the echo of starved cattle.
The ocean played with the beach
like a psychopath with his daughter.

Cirrus clouds gathered
to signal the next onslaught
as long shadows stretched inland
and caressed the lonely plains.

I returned home to a dank cottage
past the handball alley
with its political slogans
and Curran drunk in the rain

tired waiting for his uncle's death;
to a little girl playing
in the tall weeds of a railway garden.
No sun ray shone brighter

than your first gaze that evening.
You were the blackbird singing
on a headstone in the January storm,
the crocus peeping through

giving us the long awaited all clear.
Memories of you rob the howl
from the black dog when we die at night
and send the rain back to the heavens.

Memories of Bordeaux

On this wet November night
Atlantic gales wash the streets.
A gutter drips outside my window
to puncture that childhood nocturne.
The last taxi has left
from the Salthill discos
and the seagulls allow themselves
to be swept in
over the converted ballroom.
We filter to cold bedsits,
filling the pint of water
to be left on the physics book
for the thirst before dawn --
that hideous time when
hell itself could be outside.

I met Nicole last year
in the aroma of an autumn evening.
We filled trailers of grapes,
smoked Gitanes, listened
to Planxty's 'West Coast of Clare' —
compliments of the Chilean —
and the sonic boom
of the low-flying French fighters.

We gathered at the communal dinner,
almost matured into a Renoir scene
and as the dying embers
reflected in the empty wine glasses
we neutralised the voltage.

Later, speechless on a Bordeaux strand,
a fog coming from the savage Atlantic,
I felt the chill of the landscape
between Claremorris and Ballyhaunis
as seen from the first train to Dublin.
Like the scissors of two jets
in the sky over Erris we diverged.
Must I always carry a black top coat
on a summer day?

The Caretaker

For years now they've made me feel
like a ticket seller in a remote Siberian town
where the train has long ceased to stop.
But every day I live in hope
that it may slow down enough
for me to conclude a transaction.
After the train passes — at six minutes past eight
I can relax and bring herself
up a cup of coffee
and admire the summer flow
into the poisoned Kora-Bogaz
before fishing on the Lena.
Then around eleven we have coffee
on the edge of Lake Issyk Kul
before dashing off to Irkutsk for lunch.
The rest of the day is spent
I'm afraid — painting a flat
for the mistress in Vladivostok.
When they present myself and the missus
with a watch and a bouquet of flowers
after 40 years of faithful availability
I may have a thing or two to say
about the difficulty of selling tickets
to passengers in a hurry.

Lightning Source UK Ltd.
Milton Keynes UK
03 December 2009

147016UK00001B/5/P